I KISSED CLINICAL MEDICINE GOODBYE

I KISSED CLINICAL MEDICINE GOODBYE

A Guide for Physicians
Who Want to Pivot to
a Non-Clinical Career

Terralon Cannon Knight, MD

publish
y⊚ur gift

For Cannon, Allison, and Jackson.
Everything I do, I do for you.

Table of Contents

Acknowledgments

I am eternally grateful to my family for your unconditional love and unwavering support. Thank you to all who raised me, some not related by blood, but loved me (and disciplined me) just the same.

Thank you to all my teachers and professors who took an interest in me and were just as invested in me reaching my goals. My mother, Lorene, was my first teacher, and my father, Terry, and bonus mom, Caroline, remain my Sunday School teachers to this day! Thank you, and I love you!

Special thanks to Dr. Richard McGinnis, my professor and pre-medical advisor at Tougaloo College, who handed me my application to Brown University and told me I was going to apply, rather than giving me a choice.

Special thanks to Dr. Draion Burch, my business coach, who pushed me beyond my limiting thoughts to make this book possible and continues to encourage me to dream bigger.

And lastly, a special thank you to everyone who has poured into me, prayed for me, and supported me in any way. Your contributions to my life are manifesting in ways I never dreamed.

Thank you!

Preface

I love my hometown. It's a place where people still say hello and ask you how your mama is doing in the same sentence. Take a slow drive down Main Street past a combination of dated shops, the old county courthouse, a few antebellum homes, and some abandoned buildings and you might get the impression that it's an old, sleepy country town. The sole traffic light that only blinks red probably doesn't help. But don't be fooled. Our town comes alive every Friday night in the fall to rally around the county high school football team. We have years of winning seasons under our belt. Saturday mornings, highlights can be discussed play by play in any beauty or barber shop, the grocery store, or the dollar store. Sunday mornings, we might even take up a collection at church to send the team to the state championship. Our homecomings will rival any college homecoming celebration. Then, in the spring, we do it all over again for high school basketball. You see, those same kids play basketball too.

I come from a place where excellence is celebrated and champions are made. A champion is not just someone who wins at sports, but someone who is the best in their field. We understand that championships don't just happen by chance. They take hard work, persistence, and grit. So, I grew up with this winning attitude, or the resolve to win at any goal I set in life. One could say that I was groomed to have the heart of a champion while coming of age in Mississippi. More importantly, I learned that championships are not won for the team, they are for the entire community. When the team wins, the entire county wins which brings recognition, notoriety, and other opportunities we might not otherwise be afforded.

My community is just as staunchly supportive when any of its native sons or daughters champions another field of expertise. When I left to pursue my dream of becoming a doctor, there was no shortage of cheerleaders in my corner. So naturally, when I graduated from Tougaloo College and went on to Brown University for medical school, I carried the pride of my hometown with me. And when I finally graduated from medical school as Dr. Terralon Cannon, my picture appeared in the local newspaper. I was proud to share my accomplishments with the community that raised me. After all, it was another example of the hard work, persistence, and grit that produces so many other champions from the same place.

I went on to finish my family medicine residency at the University of Texas at Houston. I chose family medicine as a specialty because it allowed me to take care of a variety of patients. I always say, "I am trained for care from the womb to the tomb." I enjoyed the versatility of cases from delivering babies and seeing them for their first check-up, to seeing young adolescents for their well exams, to counseling a young grandmother about her hypertension. I even learned enough medical Spanish to conduct entire medical visits independent of an interpreter.

But after practicing for a few years, I had a secret...I didn't love medicine as much anymore. Somewhere along the way, while I was in the business of caring for patients, medicine had become just that, a business. I was spending more time charting than with my patients. Many of their treatment plans were dictated by their insurance, or lack thereof. My patients' problem lists grew, but I was being asked to shorten my time with each patient in order to see more of them. During a fifteen-minute visit, I was expected to preview the chart; interview, examine, and diagnose the patient; document a treatment plan; and complete any prescriptions, referrals, or follow-up orders. Sounds completely reasonable, right? I think it actually took me longer than fifteen minutes just to type the previous sentence! This works—well, almost never—especially since any number of scenarios can occur, including late patients, double-booked patients, and emergencies. With newer pressures to produce and more attention paid to numbers rather than quality, I invented internal time signals to help myself move in and out of patient rooms to meet productivity expectations. It got to a point as if I could hear the clock ticking every time I entered a patient's room. It ticked louder and louder the longer the visit lasted. As the ticking got louder, my heart rate simultaneously increased. All of those internal signals started feeling more like alarms…alarms too distracting to concentrate fully on my patient. I often wore comfortable flats to work, but I felt like I needed skates.

I needed a change. But what would people think? Especially people back home? I no longer felt like I was winning. I did not want to disappoint family and people who had supported me all of those years. How would I explain this decision to them? Would their pride turn to disappointment? Would they understand that I wanted to be a doctor—just in a different capacity, even if I did not see patients face-to-face every day or even at all? If I left clinical medicine, would they understand that I was still contributing to the greater good of healthcare? The guilt of my decision weighed on me heavily. I was consumed by thoughts of what others might think. The days became increasingly stressful as I struggled with the possibility of change more and more. Then, the decision became abundantly clear.

One day, during my third year of practice, the clinic day started out routinely. I had a full day of patients scheduled—children and adults, sick and well. Later in the afternoon, the patients and staff reported a malodorous aroma that soon consumed the clinic; the source seemed to stem from outside. Staff workers at the neighboring charity and bystanders on the street all agreed it smelled like gas. We evacuated the clinic, and I called our supervisors at the clinic headquarters, as we were a satellite site. We also called the local gas company. After a while, the representatives from the gas company arrived and we waited for them to clear the building. The gas company workers found no evidence of a gas leak and could not identify any other source of the smell. However, the offensive odor strongly resembling a gaseous smell consumed the clinic. I expressed my concern with practicing under those conditions to the powers that be. Not only was the smell distracting, but it was still potentially unhealthy since we were not sure what it was. It continued to consume our senses. Moreover, I was pregnant with my first child, so I did not want to take any chances with the unknown. The gas company had limited authority to confirm the presence or absence of gas. They did not look for any other source from which the odor could be coming; however, the smell was so bad and so strong it appeared to be a warning sign that could not be ignored. Nevertheless, in no uncertain terms, my leadership made it clear that since no gas leak was found, business was to continue as usual. However, due to my discomfort, my supervisor gave me the choice to leave. I made my decision that day. I canceled the rest of my patients, asking them not to come in for their safety. I knew that I could no longer practice medicine that way, at least clinically, or do business as usual.

I completed the few months left in my contract, but I did not renew with that company. After maternity leave, I made family a top priority. I found that as a family physician, there were a variety of job options available to me. And once I decided that family was my focus, I sought positions that fit a family lifestyle and designed a schedule that was family-friendly. I initially worked part-time as a school health physician, taking urgent care shifts. I eventually added part-time health center days. Unfortunately, the school health position was grant funded and it only lasted six months. It was a fun position that included educating adolescents without the previous pressures I experienced to produce. However, the productivity pressure monster soon reared its ugly head with the urgent care and clinic positions. This time, I recognized it quickly. I also decided a different change was in order. Einstein said, "The definition of insanity is doing the same thing over and over again, but expecting different results." So, if I did not want to have to buy skates, I needed to try something different. Totally different. Not just change jobs but change course completely.

The next part of my journey is not neat or straightforward. I did not have a plan or anyone to guide me with next steps. I remember having a desperate feeling to find something different to do with my skills. Something that would be a good fit. Something family friendly. And because we do not work for free, something that pays well. I started feverishly doing internet searches for other careers you could do with a medical degree. I also began to read job descriptions for anyone looking for an MD or family physician. I stumbled upon one for a medical director and a position for a young health informatics company. I met the qualifications. It was local. I had no idea what the position meant and no experience in health informatics, but I did meet the basic qualifications and I was drawn to the job description over and over again. I was going for it!

My application was accepted and I was invited for a round of interviews. After a successful round of interviews, we agreed it was a great fit for both parties and I accepted the offer! I would be learning new skills in an emerging field in healthcare. I would be the first African-American medical director to be hired. I was receiving a significant bump in pay. My commute was shorter. One new downside was that I would no longer be seeing patients. This would be my first full-time non-clinical position.

So, I thought of the people in my hometown. What would they think? Would the feelings of guilt return as I had now completely changed my course from traditional medicine? I imagine many physicians feel this way. I also imagine that the guilt of leaving clinical medicine actually causes them to stay in the positions that make them unhappy. I decided, however, that whether others understood or not, it was important for my health, well-being, and my family to make the change. I also decided that I owed it to myself to see where this new and utterly different path would take me. Therefore, I had to see myself as a champion before others would.

Champions aren't just those who take home the first-place trophy. Champions are the ones who continue to strive to be the best in their field of service, not just for themselves, but for others.

So, I am learning to reinvent myself. I am evolving. I am Dr. Terralon Cannon Knight, board-certified family physician, speaker, author, and career transition coach. I help women in the medical profession make pivotal career changes in order to create more freedom, flexibility, and financial independence.

Chapter 1
Why Change Careers?

I am excited to write this book for you. When I decided to make changes that would take my medical career in a different direction, I did not have a plethora of resources to guide me through the transition. I also did not know any people who transitioned away from clinical medicine, unless it was for retirement. For many, leaving clinical medicine for a non-clinical career was not only foreign but illogical.

I have shared my story and the factors that led to why I needed to charter a new path for myself in medicine. However, there is a myriad of reasons why others may want or need to make changes to their original career plans. For now, let us explore them in broad categories.

DESIRE TO LEARN A NEW SKILL

Believe it or not, most people like a challenge at work. Work that challenges us keeps us engaged. It also sharpens problem-solving skills. At most jobs, there is a learning curve in the beginning. And depending on your job, your personality, and opportunities that occur throughout your tenure, your interests may wax and wane. It is when the learning stops and we reach a plateau that we begin to feel bored, less interested, and eventually, stuck. The work begins to feel mundane and at times forced. Our creativity and quality of work eventually suffer.

Earlier in my career as a family physician, I loved spending time with patients. As the administrative demand for time grew, the result was less time spent with my patients. There was also one other unexpected result—my administrative duties included frequent conversations with physicians who worked for the insurance company. They seemed to be aware of a different set of rules and spoke a language I had not learned in medical school. I was slowly realizing that medicine was a business. I had gone to medical school, but not business school. And to my recollection and dismay, there had been no overlap of the two in my training. First, I discovered that physicians could work for an insurance company. Second, I needed to understand this new language. So, learning the business of medicine became a viable option for me.

DESIRE FOR MORE RESPONSIBILITY

Employees not only need to feel valued on their jobs, but they also need to be reminded of the value they bring. It is often said that the reward for good work is more work. Most employees welcome that, as it shows that the supervisor appreciates the quality of the work and trusts the employee with greater responsibility, and perhaps autonomy. Such added responsibility encourages creativity and empowerment. More responsibilities also set one on the path for career advancement. A LinkedIn survey from 2015 showed that 45 percent of individuals who recently switched jobs did so because they were concerned about the lack of opportunities for advancement.

> *"Hey, I started out mopping the floor just like you guys. But now…now I'm washing lettuce. Soon I'll be on fries; then the grill. In a year or two, I'll make assistant manager, and that's when the big bucks start rolling in."*

That is a comical statement from Maurice to Prince Akeem and Semmi from the cult classic *Coming to America*. However, we should all exhibit Maurice's ambition for growth and opportunity. I can remember as far back as age sixteen when I was hired as a cashier at my first job at the local Texaco in my hometown. As soon as I mastered my job as a cashier, I wanted to learn opening and closing procedures, which were usually reserved for more senior employees who had worked there for years. So even as a young employee, I was looking for growth opportunities.

The Bureau of Labor Statistics reported in its 2020 Employee Tenure Survey that the median tenure, or the time spent in a job before transitioning to another, was four years for women. The median tenure for men in

2018 was 4.3 years.[1] The median tenure is even shorter for millennials, which is about two years. So, the younger the employee, the more likely they are to job-hop.

NEED FOR LESS RESPONSIBILITY

Occasionally, life events cause us to shift the order of importance of our job responsibilities. Marriage, divorce, expanding a family with children, caring for elderly parents, caring for sick family members, or developing a temporary or chronic disability are just some of the circumstances that affect work schedules in a major way. If employers are inflexible or no longer able to accommodate the employee and his or her work schedule, then employees leave in search of careers with more flexibility. They also look for jobs that may offer additional benefits that support their new lifestyle, such as childcare, elder care support, disability insurance, and the option for prepaid legal services.

Because physicians are healers, they are often thought of as superhuman. However, we forget that these very real scenarios can occur in our lives as well. In 2015, Harvard Medical School and the BMJ published a survey of 250,000 medical professionals that showed the divorce rate among physicians was 22.1 percent, 22.9 percent among dentists, 21.5 percent among pharmacists, and 37.0 percent among nurses.[2] The study helped debunk the myth that physicians had higher rates of divorce than other professionals and the general public. However, female physicians were one and a half times more likely to be divorced than male physicians. There was a direct correlation between the number of hours the female physician worked and her likelihood of being divorced. Moreover, divorced female physicians reported having to make more adjustments to work responsibilities due to family commitments. With the ratio of female to male divorced physicians, one might question the support available for female physicians vs. males when there is a major life-event.

YOU WANT A CAREER THAT ALIGNS WITH YOUR CORE VALUES

As we grow and mature, our priorities and perspectives change. Whether they are clearly defined or not, we develop core values that are important both personally and professionally. Our core values guide our thoughts, behaviors, and daily decisions. They define who we are. In recent years, more individuals are searching for careers that align better with their core values. So, if your values include service, hard work, and community, you may want a career that allows outreach and community service. You may want to work for an organization that has a charitable mission. Most organizations list their core values on their website, so it should be easy to see if they align with yours.

Changing careers can be scary, but it can be done. The average person changes careers at least six times in his or her lifetime. Passions and priorities evolve, so career choices should evolve with them. Change can be uncomfortable but embrace it. We learn and grow through new experiences.

Chapter 2
Changing Your Mindset

Ask any doctor today why they became a doctor, and they will tell you it was because they wanted to help people. With medicine there is a sense of altruism, service, and nobility. Medicine utilizes science to prevent, diagnose, and treat disease. Those that practice medicine are seen as healers held in high regard. So, it can be a difficult decision when a physician decides to change careers.

I first fell in love with medicine as a young preteen. I had been having headaches for a few years and they had begun to affect me more frequently and more severely. My mother took me to the "new" doctor in town. By "new" I mean, the doctor would only be there for the next three years, as I lived in what was considered a medically underserved area and our town received physicians through the Public Health Service. That was when I met my Dr. D. She was the first African-American and first female physician I had ever seen. She listened to me, diagnosed my migraines, and educated me, all in the same visit. That encounter opened up a whole new world for me. That was over 30 years ago. Ever since that day, it was my mission to become a physician.

Many of my colleagues have similar stories. We have that one encounter that sets us on the straight and narrow path to becoming a doctor. We do not entertain any other career choices or any college majors that are not pre-med related. That's it. Do not pass go, do not collect $200.00. Many of us are so focused, we do not take time off. We follow the formula: High School + College + Medical School = MD (Internship + Residency).

For some, the formula leads to a life of service, prosperity, balance, and even the notoriety for which they were searching. However, for others, the formula may no longer work due to changes in the doctor's life or in the doctor.

Too often, there is shame when a doctor considers an alternative to traditional clinical medicine. The shame may stem from external or internal sources.

When the formula no longer fits, the doctor should be equipped to make the necessary changes to live a fulfilling life. S/he can live fearlessly knowing that they define the title, not the other way around.

In 2009, I was pregnant with my second child while working as a family physician in a clinic and also taking occasional shifts in an urgent care center. I decided that my lifestyle would no longer allow the time and flexibility I wanted to spend with my growing family; therefore, it was time to change. I needed a plan that would allow me to change my life to fit my primary goal, which was to spend more time with family while being paid a fair wage for my work. In order to do that, I had to develop and maintain a growth mindset.

DEVELOPING A GROWTH MINDSET

Western medicine has many societal pressures associated with it. There is also the large price tag--the number of years of education. And if you are an underrepresented minority, there is the added pressure of being the pride of your community. For these reasons, physicians face immense scrutiny, internally and externally, if they change careers. Therefore, having a mindset that allows the freedom and fortitude to define the next steps of one's career is essential.

Mindset is simply how you see yourself and how you see the world based on your values. Our mindset is the single most important tool that helps us determine how we should handle experiences and opportunities. In order to overcome any fear or apprehension of changing careers in or away from traditional medicine, one must have a growth mindset. A growth mindset, as defined by Carol Dweck, is one in which a person believes that new skills can be learned over time. A growth mindset is in direct contrast to a fixed mindset, which is believing one is born with all of the talent and abilities s/he is meant to have. A growth mindset allows one to see possibilities as limitless.

A growth mindset is when individuals believe talents can be developed. Fixed mindset individuals believe that talents are innate. Having a growth mindset works best for individuals who are considering a career change. As Dweck describes in the *Harvard Business Review*, they worry less about looking smart while putting more energy into learning. Individuals who are transitioning into a new career will need to learn not only new skills, but also new policies and new company culture.

Stanford psychologist Dr. Carol Dweck is renowned for her groundbreaking work on mindset. She found that our perception of ourselves and the way we see the world profoundly affects the decisions we make in life, and thus, our successes and failures. Mindset affects personal and professional relationships, behavior, and one's disposition or capacity to be happy.

Dr. Dweck found that we can manifest two contrasting mindsets from childhood––fixed or growth. One with a fixed mindset believes that she is born with innate gifts and talents that do not need further development because they are already enough to make her successful. The fixed mindset tends to be risk-averse, avoiding failure at all costs. When those with a fixed mindset encounter a setback, they tend to give up easily, believing there is nothing else to do or that alternative results are not worth the extra effort. Because a fixed mindset has static ideals, she rarely accepts constructive criticism or advice to improve a process. She is concerned with appearing intelligent more than learning a new skill, information, or ways to increase knowledge. She is threatened by others who are intelligent and successful. Those with fixed mindsets may reach some level of success but may plateau early and may not reach their full potential.

In contrast, the growth mindset encompasses the belief that our skills and talents can be further developed to meet our goals. The growth mindset is not afraid to fail forward. She uses failures as opportunities to learn and improve. She thrives on challenges and persists despite setbacks. She does not give up easily. She understands that reaching a desired goal or particular level of success takes effort, more education, working longer hours, training harder, building stronger relationships, etc. One with a growth mindset can actually celebrate the success of others and gain inspiration from their journeys.

In one of Dr. Dweck's studies, students, mostly adolescents, were given a nonverbal IQ test with ten questions. The majority of the students performed well. Dweck and her colleagues then scripted responses to theoretically push students into fixed and growth mindsets by praising one group for ability, while the other group was praised for effort.

Response One: "Wow, you got [X many] right. That's a really good score. You must be smart at this."

Response Two: "Wow, you got [X many] right. That's a really good score. You must have worked really hard."

In the next phase of the study, all of the students were given a more challenging set of problems. The students had lower performing scores on the second set of problems. As a result, the ability-praised students began to reject the idea that they were smart, while the effort-praised students accepted their results as an indication that more effort was needed, rather than a sign of deficiency in their intelligence. The difference in mindsets continued to manifest. During the first set of problems, all of the students seemed to express enjoyment. However, the ability-praised students, who had clearly adopted a fixed mindset, expressed more dissatisfaction with the second, more challenging set of problems. The effort-praised students demonstrated a growth mindset by not only their enjoyment of the second set of problems, but also expressed that the more challenging, the more fun. It also appeared that as the problems became more challenging, the ability-praised students became more discouraged which negatively impacted their performance. Conversely, the effort-praised group showed improvements in performance.

In the concluding portion of the testing phase, Dweck and her colleagues asked the students to write letters to their peers detailing their experiences, including their scores. An unexpected and concerning result included 40 percent of the ability-praised students lying about their scores by raising them to look more successful. "In the fixed mindset, imperfections are shameful—especially if you're talented—so they lied them away. What's so alarming is that we took ordinary children and made them into liars, simply by telling them they were smart." The fixed mindset detested challenge and saw failure as final and shameful. Thus, there were limits to their achievements. The growth mindset showed persistence when faced with challenges, and perceived failure as opportunity.

Mindset is the single most important factor in decision-making. As we embark on the important topic of career transition, it is essential for you to understand which mindset you currently have. If you have a growth mindset, you are well on your way to a successful future, no matter which path you choose. For if your next venture takes a little more time, more effort, or does not work as anticipated, you will not see it as a failure but as a learning opportunity, and likely a springboard to a subsequent venture. However, if you have a fixed mindset, congratulations on identifying that. (We celebrate all wins here! It's part of my growth mindset!)

Now that you have acknowledged your fixed mindset, let us identify what changes are needed to move to a growth mindset.

1. First, it is important to understand that science backs the growth mindset. Neuroplasticity was introduced in 1998. It is the science that explains how the brain forms new neural pathways as it learns a new skill. For example, as you learn a new skill, such as knitting, the neural pathways begin to form. The more you practice knitting, more myelin is produced along the pathways. Myelin is the material that insulates the nerve, allowing the signal to travel faster along the neuron. As more neural pathways are produced, more myelin is produced, and the brain gets stronger. Neuroplasticity debunks the belief that the brain completes development in childhood. Therefore, you must first believe that it has been scientifically proven that you can master a new skill.

2. Surround yourself with others who have a growth mindset. You know these people. They are the ones who tend to see the glass half-full when faced with any challenge, large or small. In fact, the challenges seem to motivate them to work

harder. In their eyes, setbacks are merely opportunities to reevaluate, and become more creative and strategic. They are rarely selfish, believing their wins benefit others and that success is best shared. Remember the friend who never gets frustrated when close parking is not available. In fact, the farther away the spot, the greater the opportunity to meet her step goal for the day. And it is a plus if she gets you to exercise with her. You want her and others like her on your team. Positive attitudes are contagious. The more you associate with others who think and speak with a growth mindset, you will subconsciously and consciously take on the characteristics of your environment.

3. Embrace imperfection. While we know we are not all perfect, it is the fixed mindset that is ashamed of and tries to hide imperfection. Therefore, acknowledge your imperfection. Then, change your perception. Celebrate it as your own unique calling card. Much of what we dislike about ourselves is shaped by societal norms. However, societal norms and what is accepted change over time. In other words, people are flaky. So, it is important that you are pleased

with yourself. As a child, Cindy Crawford was teased about the "dot" above the left corner of her upper lip. Her mother discouraged her from having it removed. It is now an iconic beauty mark that is synonymous with Crawford, which was a factor in launching her thirty-plus year beauty career.

4. Focus more on the process than the end result. The process is where true growth occurs. Concentrating on the methods allows opportunity for learning and understanding. The fixed mindset focuses on outcome. However, if you take time to learn and understand the process, chances for success that can be replicated and scaled are increased. Tennis great Arthur Ashe once said, "Success is a journey, not a destination. The doing is often more important than the outcome."

5. Never stop learning. Become curious about everything. Ask more questions about things that are unfamiliar, but also ask questions about ideas which you believe you know a great deal. You might be surprised what you learn. "I have no special talents. I am just passionately curious," said Albert Einstein.

LESSONS FROM A HOUSEPLANT

My mother has quite the green thumb. She says she inherited it from her grandmother. It obviously skips a generation in our family. I don't recall her mother, my maternal grandmother, having many plants. Likewise, I can't seem to remember to water the plants my mother gives me. However, when you enter my mother's home, office, or any space she frequents, expect to navigate through ficus trees, rubber plants, hanging baskets, and a number of perennial flowering plants. She even manages to keep a vegetable garden, on some scale year-round, thanks to the temperate climate in Mississippi.

My mother has helped me with almost every move after high school. I really needed her for the decorating, because truth be told, I have no style. And if my mother is involved, no space is complete without, you guessed it, a plant. With her vast knowledge of horticulture, my mother found the one plant I could not kill.

The pothos plant goes by many names: devil's ivy, the money plant, marble queen, and silver vine. It is a beautiful, evergreen plant that has heart-shaped leaves but rarely flowers. It grows well in low light, which makes it an ideal plant for a dormitory room or dimly lit apartment. It can go days without being watered, so it is very medical student, exhausted medical resident, or busy-person-in-general friendly. It can also grow in soil or propagate well in a container of water, as long as there is water in the container.

My mother gave me my last pothos plant during finals of my third year in medical school at Brown University in 2000. Not the greatest idea to move during finals, but Mommy to the rescue! I left to study. I returned to a fully organized and decorated apartment, complete with her signature houseplant. I am sure I forgot to water it plenty of times, but it lasted the next two years in Rhode Island in my basement apartment. That houseplant lasted through graduation and moved with me to Houston, Texas, where I trained as a family medicine resident. I shared my next apartment with a roommate, another physician further along than me in her training, and therefore, busier than I.

My pothos had a nice home in the living room with lots of indirect sunlight near the window of our second-story apartment. It was our only plant, but as I remember, we still forgot to water it. There were no strict limits on resident work hours, such as the ACGME's 80-hour work week rule currently in place. So, it was not uncommon for us to neglect the plant a week or so at a time due to hours long shifts at the hospital alternating with time spent at home mostly sleeping.

After the first year, I purchased my first home. My mom helped decorate at some point, most likely while I was at the hospital. It also meant time for special attention to my plant. It had experienced growth, but we were in a new environment and a new climate, and my mom needed to ensure that the plant would continue to grow well in its new surroundings. So, she trimmed dead leaves and pruned leggy branches that were not producing. She also exchanged the soil for new fertile soil and repotted it into a larger pot. The pruning and repotting appeared to breathe new life into my little plant over the remaining two years in Houston.

After residency, marriage took me to Maryland with a job in nearby Washington, DC. My plant got a new home in a cozy foyer with lots of natural light. I remembered to water it a bit more regularly. That lasted only until our first child came. By now, the plant was eight years old, and I had reverted to its original watering schedule, which was almost never. That was mainly because with a new baby, I was back to my medical school and residency memory and sleep schedule. My mother came for a visit, but for the first time, the plant would have to wait. In a fight for attention between daughter's first baby vs. plant, plant loses every time.

In 2010, we moved again to another house and added a new child to the family. The pothos was moved to the solarium. It had more light than ever before. It was time for Mommy to come, again. This time, since I was no longer a first-time mom, she fit in time for grandchildren and gardening inside and outside! My pothos was repotted. This time the vine was actually shaped and "trained" to climb along certain paths along the tops of the windows, while other branches suspended horizontally outside of the pot. And, of course, nonproductive branches were pruned, leggy leaves were cut, and brown leaves were removed.

As life continued to get busier with the addition of a third child and increased work responsibilities, I still only managed to remember to water the plant occasionally as did others in my home. The solarium was not a room we spent lots of time in and the pothos was our only plant. Still, somehow the pothos faithfully grew. If you're counting, my pothos lasted twenty years, three states, five homes, the birth of three children, and four repottings. For the first time ever after repotting, the soil was found to have parasitic insects that destroyed the plant. It was an unfortunate fluke for a strong, resilient plant. However, the good news is that my mother was able to take a branch and place it in a container of water. She knew that the pothos plant easily propagates in water, so all was not lost.

WHAT CAN WE LEARN FROM THE POTHOS PLANT?

It is evergreen.

To be an evergreen individual, one must stay relevant. How does one stay relevant? You stay relevant by absorbing and retaining as much information about your chosen career and interests as possible. Read and network with experts in your chosen field. Practice your craft as often as possible. If your passion is patient care, continuously research innovative ways to improve the patient outcomes in medicine. If your passion is baking, perfect your sourdough bread by experimenting with different recipes, or even take a group class. No matter the interest, strive to be the best and remain current.

It thrives in low light.

The pothos plant grows well in ample light or in dimly lit areas. It continues to produce and expand as long as water is provided to the root system. Sometimes hard work and, therefore, success are not recognized immediately. This should not deter us from working toward our goals. Recognition and praise should never be benchmarks for success. Many will not understand your purpose, especially if it is unconventional. Let your passion be your motivating force to keep working toward your goals. Learn to celebrate yourself and your smaller wins along the journey to your ultimate goals. As someone put it, "Hustle in silence and let success be the noise."

It adapts easily.

Because the pothos plant can grow in low light or well-lit areas, it is highly adaptable. You may recall my houseplant survived three different dwellings, in three climates including New England, the Southwest, and the Mid-Atlantic, over a twenty-year span. And in those twenty years, my responsibilities impacted its care and attention. Nevertheless, it not only survived, but it continued to grow. Changes in life are inevitable. Some are positive and propel us further in the direction we want to go. Other changes may set us back or cause us to question our choices. When such changes occur, we must go back and review our purpose, our unique assignment for being here on Earth. We must ensure the purpose is clear. Once the purpose is clear, we must adjust the plans to accommodate the change. Remember that the branches of the plant can continue to grow horizontally and downward, but vines can also be "trained" to grow upward. Passion can still be used to cultivate the new course of direction to reach the same goal. In essence, the purpose and passion did not change, only the plans.

An ophthalmologist serves her patients faithfully through her clinical practice, outpatient visits, and minor eye surgeries. One day, without warning, she feels numbness and tingling in her right hand. As the days progress, she begins to drop objects. Dr. Smith decides to get a full evaluation. The diagnosis is carpal tunnel syndrome. The decision is made that she will no longer perform surgical procedures after her own surgery. And because she will no longer perform surgery, she will close her clinic in which she saw patients for pre-operative visits. The diagnosis is life-changing, but not career-ending. Dr. Smith takes the time while recovering from surgery to revisit her purpose. She is still passionate about caring for her patients. She still loves the anatomy of the eye. Dr. Smith knows that she still needs to continue to work to maintain an income, as she has a family and financial obligations. Dr. Smith desires to create a new career that encompasses all of the things she loved about her career prior to her surgery. After further reflection with a coach, Dr. Smith realizes that she found the most joy when educating patients about prevention and treatment of eye disease. A review of her skills also reveals that Dr. Smith is a good writer and has experience from working in journalism as a writer for her college newspaper. With guidance from her coach, Dr. Smith discovers that medical editing is likely a good next step as a career transition. Dr. Smith begins a new career as a medical editor for a medical journal focused on diseases of the eye and writing educational blog posts featuring common problems and treatments of the eye. She finds that this lifestyle serves her purpose to educate patients and fuels her passion for the study of the eye, while giving her more freedom to spend time with her family.

It is resilient.

I have neglected my houseplant more times than I can count. In times when water was scarce (not because it was ever in short supply, but simply because I forgot to water it), the pothos did not grow at peak potential. At times, it continued to grow but became leggy, growing in length but with scarce leaves and not in fullness. Sometimes, it even produced brown and yellow leaves during those lean times. However, when pruned and repotted, the plant came roaring back stronger than before. Resilience is the ability to recover quickly from adversity. When you are pursuing your purpose, the road to success is not always smooth.

Oprah Winfrey survived years of sexual abuse, the loss of a child, and being fired and labeled "unfit for TV" before becoming one of the most successful women in television and entertainment. Michael Jordan, one of the best basketball players of all time, was cut from his high school basketball team. He shared, "I have missed more than 9,000 shots in my career. I have lost almost 300 games. On 26 occasions I have been entrusted to take the game winning shot…and I missed. I have failed over and over and over again in my life. And that's precisely why I succeed."[3]

To be resilient, we must change our perspective when it comes to adversity. We must choose to see setbacks as opportunities for growth, a chance to strengthen our skill set. If we don't have the tools ourselves to solve the problem immediately, challenges may be opportunities to build our social and professional networks. By expanding our networks, we increase diversity of thought and strengthen our problem-solving skills and resources. By changing our perspective, embracing the problem, establishing a plan, and taking action, the saying holds true: "The setback was merely a setup for a comeback."

Chapter 3
Purpose, Passion, and a Plan

WHAT IS YOUR PURPOSE?

"Each of you should use whatever gift you have received to serve others, as faithful stewards of God's grace in its various forms" (1 Peter 4:10).

When considering next steps in your career path, you must first consider your purpose. It must be clear as you are making plans to create a life to accomplish your goals. Each of us has an assignment to fulfill here on Earth. We utilize our unique skill sets and talents to carry out our purpose. Some talents we are born with, while others are cultivated. When we are working in our purpose, we are meeting the need(s) of an individual or community, while receiving self-fulfillment. Many people clearly understand their purpose while others have to search for it.

If you are one of those people who already knows what your purpose is—congratulations! However, if you are one of the remaining folks who needs help with discovering your purpose, welcome! You have come to the right place! Understanding your purpose is not always straightforward.

Here are some tips to help you discover your purpose and walk confidently in it.

1. What are you good at? Think of a skill that makes you sought-after or for which you receive many compliments. Perhaps you explain confusing concepts to colleagues very well, making you a great teacher. Or perhaps you are known for your delicious homemade meals, making you a celebrity-chef among your circle of friends. Moreover, you may simply be great at listening, encouraging, and giving advice. Everyone has their own special skill set designed especially for their purpose.

2. Can this work make the lives of others better? Your purpose works not just to serve you, but to serve others and to improve the world around you. So, if your purpose is to teach, then education should fill a gap. Likewise, cooking improves the lives of others by feeding a community. And depending on the delivery of the services, both education and cooking can provide jobs.

3. Am I keeping an open mind? Many people have the idea that they were meant to do one thing in life. That they were meant for one purpose. However, as we gain new skills and sharpen old ones,

we become positioned to be more versatile. And much like the pothos plant, we can adapt to meet a vastly changing world. Therefore, it is possible to accomplish more than one purpose simultaneously. Or perhaps, as skills and talents develop over time, so does our purpose.

4. What do my friends, family, and colleagues say? Getting the perspective of others is valuable. It is always interesting to see how others see us. You may be pleasantly surprised by strengths others see in you that you did not see in yourself. Warning: only ask those who will give supportive, insightful feedback.

WHAT IS YOUR PASSION?

Passion can be thought of as strong feelings of positive emotions. If your current job or career does not spark joy, then it is time to create a transition plan. First, evaluate if you are living and working in your true purpose, as outlined above. Then, decide if you are passionate about the work. If you are not, begin your new transition plan with passion and purpose at the forefront, understanding that any next career will not be fulfilling without them.

For tips to further identify your passion, see below.

1. What type of work would you do for free? Think of the type of work you would do if money were

not a factor, but it still gave you endless satisfaction. Think of the type of emotion you got from building with Lego blocks or playing with dolls for hours (if only we could get paid for that now).

2. What do you spend hours thinking about? Think about the things from childhood until now that you spend time dreaming about. Are there articles or books on a subject that you tend to gravitate to and then recreate, like interior design or crafting? Hobbies, such as travel, can also be passions. Activities that inspire and excite you have the potential to become career opportunities.

3. Is there a pain point that has become a passion? Many times, we do not realize it, but the things that motivate us the most are the things that frustrate us the most. Perhaps there is a political issue or a problem at your current job that has propelled you into a position to lead the charge for change. Therefore, your new mission is your new passion. A physician colleague noticed a lack of women in tenured positions at her institution. This led to educational workshops to raise awareness and review the process. The workshop has now grown into a three-day conference with national speakers, which sells out each year.

4. What do friends, family, and colleagues say? Ask them to share with you their perception of what excites you or what makes you happy. Sometimes it helps to see ourselves through the eyes of others. I had a client practice this exercise with her loved ones. She was surprised to learn that a common response was cooking. While she knew she enjoyed cooking and felt it was a necessary activity of daily living, she was surprised to learn that others could see the joy that cooking brought her. As a result, she is now considering a certification in culinary medicine.

MAKE A PLAN

You have identified your purpose. You have identified your passion. Now it is time to make a plan of action.

EVALUATE YOUR CURRENT POSITION

Evaluate your current position to see if it aligns with your purpose and passion. If your career is not in alignment, identify which changes are needed to make it more fulfilling. You will need to identify whether there are logistical changes that need to be made at the job, such as scheduling, staff, etc. Alternatively, consider whether there simply needs to be a mindset shift. Now that your purpose and passion have been clarified, your approach to the daily routine may be different, such as more optimism or more delegation.

RESEARCH ALTERNATIVE CAREERS

If the current position does not align with your passion and your purpose, begin to research and identify the kinds of careers that would allow you to carry out your passion and purpose. Be creative, be open, and be optimistic. Also, do not be afraid to cast a wide net. Talk to friends and colleagues who share some of the same interests. Look within your professional network. In addition, one job might not meet your needs, so be flexible and even consider multiple jobs simultaneously if time allows. With positions offering virtual alternatives, coupled with the ability to recycle content over different media, there are opportunities to juggle multiple passions at a time. For instance, one can be a travel blogger, speaker, virtual teacher, and podcaster all at the same time.

MAKE A LIST OF YOUR MUST-HAVES

Chances are if you are at the stage in your life where you are considering making changes in your professional career, there are personal values that strongly impact your choices. For the most part, our early years in education and training are prescriptive as we formulate our ideas about what we want to be "when we grow up." The American standard of elementary school, middle school, and high school tend to follow the same formula nation-wide. However, our values and interests are developing simultaneously, making each of our experiences unique. This would explain why two friends from the same town who attended the same schools became pediatricians and even partners in the same practice.

After five years, Dana decides that she likes her work but does not feel the same joy she previously felt when they started the practice in their hometown and has felt increasingly dissatisfied. Angela, on the other hand, still enjoys her work just as much and even has new ideas about how to expand the practice. Dana would like to start a family soon and would like more time to spend with her aging father. Angela also wants to spend less time performing direct patient care in the clinic her-self. However, she would like to bring in more mid-level providers, such as physician assistants and nurse prac-titioners to serve more patients. This will allow Angela to pursue leadership positions at the local hospital and teach at the medical school.

Two women who followed the same professional ca-reer path have divergent interests at five years in. Dana needs to create a lifestyle that accommodates time for an expanding family and the care of an aging parent. An-gela needs to create a lifestyle that will accommodate a growing practice and time for leadership responsibilities. While one prepares to decrease work responsibilities for family and the other prepares to scale up for practice growth, neither value is more important or less valuable. Each woman is running her own unique race. Adjusting career goals to accommodate personal values and responsibilities should not be seen as an obstacle. Instead, it should be viewed as a necessity for each physician to live a fulfilling life, resulting in better service to patients.

By now, you are far enough along in your career to decide what your pleasure and pain points are. List them. Be specific. Decide what is important at this juncture for you to be fulfilled and to serve in your purpose effectively. Decide what values cannot be compromised as you transition to your next position. It may also help to think about who will benefit from your must-haves or what else might be gained. For example, when I chose to transition from full-time clinical patient care, the decision came out of the need to spend more time with my expanding family. It was important to me to transition to a career with no more overnight calls and no more weekends (as many of my family's extracurricular activities occurred on the weekends). I desired a shorter commute, as again, time was an important factor. When thinking of who would benefit, I discovered that my family, patients, other physicians, and I would all benefit! The most obvious benefit would be to my family, as we would be afforded more time together with the career change. My position was with a relatively young start-up health IT firm in which I consulted on a variety of projects in healthcare, not limited to coding, fraud, waste, and abuse, and researching drugs for orphan diseases. So, as the healthcare community was benefitting, I was developing a new skill set.

CREATE A VISION BOARD

Proverbs 29:18 tells us, "Where there is no vision, the people perish." It is not only important to make goals, but to take the time to visualize them. Think about it. How many things do you create by hand before first creating them in your mind? Visualization is a technique that is commonly used by psychologists and others to improve performance for a desired result. The process involves seeing the outcome and simulating the steps of the process of the skill-based activity. For example, prior to a race, and especially during her training, an Olympic runner may visualize winning the race. She will also need to visually go through each of the steps from start to finish with as much detail as possible. There is a direct correlation between the amount of details in the visual images and the amount of connections between neurons that will increase motivation for performance toward the desired goal.

We must take the visualization technique a step further and memorialize it on a vision board. By making a physical reminder of our goals, we further increase our chances of manifesting the desired outcome. Take the plan you have outlined for yourself and place it on a board.

You will need: old magazines, newspapers, scissors, glue, poster/cork/foam board

There are no real rules when it comes to a vision board, except it should reflect what you want to see manifested. So far, we have focused on creating a fulfilling life based on purpose and passion. Therefore, you should choose words, pictures, and people that reflect the idea of the life you desire and people you admire. Because vision boards should encourage action, motivational quotes may be helpful. If there are hobbies you would like to try or places you have not visited yet, don't be afraid to add them to your vision board. The board should inspire you. Again, there are no rules. Also, because there are no rules, you can change out aspects of your board as often as you like or create a new one as often as you feel the need. Once complete, the vision board should be placed in an area where you will see it often to feed the necessary visual images to your brain that will motivate you to take action.

Chapter 4
Evaluate Your Health: Physical, Emotional, and Financial

Your purpose is clear. You are passionate about the coming change. You have a plan. But are you mentally and physically ready to make the change? Before walking away from your current job, it is important to pause. So far, we have looked prospectively at what we would like to see in our next position. Now, let's take a moment to look introspectively. It is important to ensure that you do not overlook key issues that may hinder success after your career transition. It is vital to assess, before walking away, if the job no longer gels with your goals, or conversely, if it is you who has changed your perspective. The latter is ok unless your perspective is clouded by a view that could also negatively affect future opportunities if not addressed.

Thankfully, there is more data, and therefore more awareness, about physician burnout now than in previous years. Burnout is described as emotional exhaustion in the workplace, which may affect performance, further characterized by negative feelings and responses to workplace stress. Everyone experiences dissatisfaction on the job from time to time. However, burnout is a pervasive, chronic state of mind that will eventually affect performance, professional and personal relationships, and professional reputation if undetected and untreated. Based on Winona State University's Burnout Study, there are five stages to burnout:

1. The Honeymoon Phase – During this time, the physician is excited about taking on new tasks, is highly committed, and experiences high job satisfaction. Normal stressors occur at this time, but they are predictable and handled well.

2. The Onset of Stress – The physician becomes less optimistic and more irritable. Productivity is lower. Physical signs of stress may begin to appear, such as increased blood pressure, lack of sleep, and fatigue.

3. Chronic Stress – The physician begins to show signs of marked stress more frequently. Physical signs of stress intensify. Physician begins to miss deadlines. S/he is repeatedly late for work and procrastinates at work and home. S/he exhibits increased morning fatigue and appears to be physically ill more often. Emotionally, s/he expresses more pessimism, apathy, and cynicism.

4. Burnout – This is the stage most discussed. Intervention is key at this stage to decrease the risk

of an emotional or physical event. Physician experiences self-doubt, hopelessness about the future, and may socially isolate. Physical symptoms intensify, such as chronic headaches and gastrointestinal issues. Physician is low functioning at work.

5. Habitual Burnout – This is the final stage of burnout. The physician is at highest risk for experiencing an emotional or physical event. Symptoms include chronic sadness or depression.

ADDRESSING BURNOUT

To address the burnout, it may not be necessary to walk completely away from the job.

First, take a break. All too often, while physicians are caring for others, we do not take the time to take care of ourselves. Take some time away from work. This means totally unplugging from work. Do not call in, do not check messages, do not check emails. At least one week, two weeks if possible, will allow you to relax the way you want to and evaluate the positives and negatives of the current job without distractions.

When you return to work, decide if there are positives at your current job that outweigh the negatives enough for you to stay, provided the negatives can be modified. Speak with your supervisor and other stakeholders to see if there is consensus on the opportunities for improvement you have identified and set a deadline. Identify whether this is a team with a growth mindset or not. If so, they will be willing to not only react to your current concerns but be proactive going forward, not waiting until you bring concerns to them.

Insert regular self-care into your routine. Burnout commonly occurs when we don't take scheduled breaks and vacations. Get plenty of rest and sleep, which are not the same. Insert relaxing activities into your routine such as meditation, yoga, or walks to decrease stress. Get regular exercise and eat right.

Form a support network with colleagues that are doing similar work that may have more experience. Find a mentor to regularly discuss ideas and from whom you can receive advice.

See a mental health specialist. All too often, symptoms of burnout overlap with depression, anxiety, or other mental health disorders. It is important to seek help as soon as possible.

PHYSICAL HEALTH EVALUATION

It is often said that physicians do not take care of themselves as well as they treat their patients. In fact, a July 21, 2017, Advisory Board study substantiated that there are a few challenges with physicians as patients. It is not that we are not going to the doctor, but it seems that our lack of open communication is causing us to receive a lower quality of care from our colleagues. One such assumption that is made is that the physician-patient discusses his or her history freely and tells the examining physician everything s/he needs to know about his or her condition to make a diagnosis. However, this does not always occur, which may lead to error in diagnosis or missed diagnosis. For example, if a patient complains of fatigue, it could be a symptom of anything from burnout, to insomnia, to obstructive sleep apnea, to depression, to thyroid disease, to anemia, to a host of other diseases. So, it's important that you provide as many details about your history as possible to help the examiner focus on a plan of treatment on the most likely cause of your symptoms.

In addition to seeing your doctor, maintain a healthy weight by eating a healthy diet. Diets heavy in carbohydrates tend to sink our moods while green, leafy vegetables and fruits lift our moods. Whole grain oats provide fiber that stabilizes our blood sugar and lifts our mood. Berries have antioxidants which fight harmful compounds in our bodies and depression.

If you're not exercising regularly, add it to your routine. If you are exercising, continue. The American Heart Association recommends at least 150 minutes of moderate-intensity aerobic activity or 75 minutes per week of vigorous aerobic activity spread throughout the week, along with two days of muscle-strengthening activity. Exercise is a natural stress reducer.

SPIRITUAL WELLNESS

Spirituality allows one to connect to a higher power and a belief system that encompasses our values that govern our everyday choices. When taking a holistic view, mental, physical, and spiritual wellness are all important and interconnected. There is evidence that spiritual wellness directly affects physical wellness. Some ways to maintain spiritual wellness include:

1. Meditation – Meditation is a relaxed state of awareness. It is an ancient practice in many cultures all over the world. It is more about finding peace than about religion.

2. Yoga – Yoga is a set of poses, breathing exercises, and meditation that originated in India 5,000 years ago. In addition to physical strength and balance, yoga improves mental clarity and calmness.

3. Affirmations – Affirmations are declarations of positivity that counteract negative, self-sabotaging thoughts. Repeat daily to change unconscious negative thinking. Also, daily affirmations will increase your motivation, much like your vision board, and keep you focused on reaching your goals.

FINANCIAL WELLNESS

Are you financially ready to quit?

So, you are ready to take the leap. You are ready to quit. I know you have been at your job several years, but what does your contract say? Do you have to give your employer a certain amount of time? Is there a noncompete clause that may prevent you from moving forward with your next venture? Read carefully. For the large print giveth, and the small print taketh away.

Pay down credit cards so that you are not carrying balances. Know your monthly expenses and trim the unnecessary expenses. Contact all three credit bureaus and address any issues with your credit report. For costs formerly handled by your employer, like health insurance and retirement savings, consider how you will handle those costs going forward.

Conventional wisdom previously called for six months living expenses for savings. However, if you are starting a business, you should also set aside at least one-quarter worth of business expenses.

If possible, secure another source of income before leaving your current job.

Review the employer-paid benefits you are receiving from your company. Paid vacation days, 401(k) plan with employer matching contributions, health insurance, and term life insurance are among the common benefits provided by companies. If you are married and your spouse works, coverage under your spouse may be an option. Also, consider purchasing insurance before you leave your current job to avoid any gaps in coverage and calculate the premiums. Check your pay stubs for any other employer-paid benefits. Make a list of benefits you would like to continue and ensure you can afford them going forward.

Determine your monthly spending plan. Do this by taking the average of the last twelve months of expenses. Jim Wang for *Forbes Magazine* writes that you should try living on your new spending plan for two months. This will help you determine whether you need to make adjustments or not. The spending plan should allow room to save for larger expenses.

Check to see if your next position includes 401(k) with matching. Compare 401(k) alternatives. If you are starting a business, research self-employed 401(k) plans.

*If the thought of crunching numbers for spending plans, budgeting, and 401k plans is too much, you may want to hire a financial advisor. As you are looking, decide whether you are looking for investment and retirement help or someone for general financial advice as needed. This will help determine whether you should work with a commission-based financial advisor or a fee-based advisor. Also consider accredited financial counselors who are often more affordable. Accredited financial counselors often specialize in topics such as saving, budgeting, and improving credit. They educate but cannot legally give advice about investments.

Finding the right financial advisor is much like finding a primary care physician. You should feel very comfortable with him or her. You will be sharing personal information, and money can be a sensitive and complex subject for some. And, depending on your financial aptitude, the financial advisor may seem to speak a different language. Therefore, you should be comfortable enough with your advisor to ask questions freely. Here are some questions to start with:

1. Can you describe your typical client?

2. How do you like to work with clients?

3. How do you prefer to communicate with your client?

4. How do you get paid? How will I be charged?

5. Are you a fiduciary?

6. How will you help me reach my goals?

7. Can you provide me with references?

Fiduciaries are legally bound to put your financial needs before their own. Look for certified financial planners, registered investment advisors, investment advisor representatives, chartered retirement planning counselors, and accredited investment fiduciaries. These positions all have fiduciary-level designation.

BEWARE OF "GOLDEN HANDCUFFS"

According to the Association of American Medical Colleges, the average medical student graduates with $201,490.00 in debt. Debt accumulated in college and medical school is the first step in the process that leads to entrapment by "golden handcuffs." "Golden handcuffs" refers to the idea that an individual is stuck in a job because of the dependence on its income in order to maintain an often-expensive lifestyle. This is a very common phenomenon among physicians, who tend to be high earners with high expenses. Also, over time, physicians have become super specialized, as Robert Kiyosaki tells us in *Rich Dad Poor Dad*. The more specialized physicians become, the more we tend to feel tied to our careers and even particular jobs. Moreover, the higher the pay, the less willing a physician is to make changes especially if s/he has accrued expenses in proportion to his or her salary. These high-earning jobs may come with big paychecks, long commutes, long hours, heavy administrative burden, little flexibility, and little autonomy. However, if the expenses are high, sometimes these pain points are not enough to offset the paycheck. The sense of financial security is too great, although the physician is essentially living check-to-check. Thus, the risk to change careers seems too great and the "golden handcuffs" continue to bind the physician to their job.

So, you think you're ready to make a change, but you're not sure how to go about it. First, review your purpose and passion. Now, make an expansive list of careers that incorporate your purpose and passion. This list should not be limited by factors such as location, previous experience, or salary. In the next step, edit the list to apply must-haves (listed in the previous chapter).

Once you have your short list, begin your research. First, look within your network. Look for individuals who are doing the jobs you are interested in. Do not be shy about asking questions. You want to know about company culture, benefits, time off, and required training. If there is a company you are particularly interested in, reach out or apply with the company directly. Also, use social media to research sites dedicated to careers in your field of interest, or specifically, the companies' social media pages. Read reviews from former employees. However, read carefully. Many negative reviews are often written by disgruntled employees who have issues that stem from disputes with another employee. Also, pay close attention to positions, titles, and location as their grievances may be isolated to a department or location. Rarely do negative reviews give you a glance of company culture unless you spot a trend.

Whether you are applying for a job or you decide to venture out on your own, determine whether you need to take a class or get a certification. Developing a new skill set may not only be necessary, but it also provides a refreshing feeling that comes with learning something new. Taking a class also offers the opportunity to expand one's network of individuals in the same field.

Take some time to review your resume. Update it as necessary with skills you acquired over the previous years at your current job. Highlight leadership tasks and major accomplishments. Depending on the job or venture, you may need multiple resumes that highlight different skills. If you are launching your own business, concentrate on branding. You may want to update head-shots, web pages, and any social media accounts. Make sure you are clear about goals and that you can state them clearly to your clients.

After you are satisfied with your resume and rebranding, go for it! Launch! The best way to know if something works is to try it.

Chapter 5
More Actions to Take

WHAT IS YOUR ONLINE PERSONA?

Evaluate all of your social media accounts. Employers perform social media screenings of candidates. According to a 2018 CareerBuilder survey, about 70 percent of employers screened the social media accounts of potential candidates. Almost 40 percent stated that they screen the social media accounts of current employees. More than 50 percent of employers stated that they found inappropriate information. Such information includes inappropriate photos; information about active substance use; and discriminatory remarks about someone of another race, gender, or culture. So, if you are struggling to decide if you should accept a friend request from former associates who participate in questionable recreational activities and love to post about it, struggle no more.

Consider making your personal account private and creating a public, professional account.

HIRE A CAREER COACH

A career coach guides you along the steps of career transition and provides accountability. S/he does not find the job for you, as s/he is not a recruiter or a headhunter. However, s/he does help tailor the process according to your skill set and interests. While not a counselor, a career coach can decrease stress by empowering and encouraging you at each step throughout the process. Sometimes, the major factor in a successful career transition is accountability. The client-coach relationship is important, as you will share intimate details of your life. Therefore, you should be comfortable with your coach. Coaching is very personalized. While you may find a coach via a referral or internet source, it is important that the coach has a style that works well to motivate you.

ALTERNATIVE CAREERS FOR PHYSICIANS TO CONSIDER
Locum tenens

Locum tenens may be just what the doctor ordered for the physician with the spirit of wanderlust. Locum tenens is a Latin phrase that means "to hold the place of." Think of it as being a substitute doctor. By working as a locum tenens doctor, a physician may choose length of assignments, location, and even the setting (inpatient, outpatient, etc.). With that type of flexibility, a physician truly can create the life s/he desires. In addition, this is one job a physician can keep as a weekend warrior, just in case s/he isn't quite ready to leave his or her current job.

TEACHING

Use your medical expertise and background in science and other areas of study to inspire a new generation. Universities, community colleges, and vocational schools are good options for physicians who enjoy education and mentoring young minds. It is also a great option to consider if one is thinking of a part-time alternative without the pressures of a research commitment.

PHYSICIAN CONSULTING

Consulting is simply getting paid for advice based on your medical expertise. Companies from large Fortune 500s to small startups are interested in the medical knowledge physicians can provide. Physician consultants have a range of responsibilities from supporting healthcare research to supporting product development. They are usually part of larger teams, but they are considered the subject matter experts (SMEs) on the teams. This can be a very lucrative career, as some private contractors can command fees upwards of $500/hour.

CORPORATE OR INSURANCE MEDICINE/ PHYSICIAN EXECUTIVE

To practicing physicians, insurance companies may sometimes seem like the big bad wolf. However, working for these companies gives one a chance to help shape policies. And since most decisions are evidence-based, physicians who work for these companies often bridge the gap between the business priorities and the medical needs of the patient. For many doctors, this position not only provides the lifestyle change for which they are searching, but also the autonomy and the satisfaction that they are shaping healthcare policies.

MEDICAL EDITING

If you have always been a savvy wordsmith, then medical editing may be for you. Medical editors are responsible for CME coursework, s blogs, and proofing journal articles. Much of the work can be done virtually and during flexible hours. Medical writing or editing can be considered part-time or full-time.

Chapter 6
Are You Smarter Than an Octopus?

My youngest son loves animal facts, so it is a good day when I can impress him by sharing an animal fact that he has never heard. I am also keenly aware that the day is coming soon when I will no longer be able to impress him at all. So, my quest to impress him serendipitously led me to research about species of octopus. I find them to be fascinating creatures. Did you know they have nine brains? Well, actually the octopus has a central brain located in its head, while each of its eight arms has a cluster of neurons. Because each cluster of neurons acts independently of the central brain, and the other arms, they are considered mini-brains. These mini-brains are responsible for movement, taste, and feel. It is as if the mini-brains give the order for the arm to move, then pass along the message to the central brain as a side note (haha!). Conversely, the human brain is the main control center and tells the hand to move after it receives a message from neurons in the hand that the stove is hot. Oversimplified illustration, but hopefully clear.

Unlike humans, octopuses lack proprioception (a sense of where their bodies are in relation to their environment). If you place your hand behind your back, you are still aware of the location of your hand. However, octopuses are only aware of the body parts that their eyes can see. Some scientists debate whether this actually lowers the octopus's defenses.

Nevertheless, there are five things we can learn from the octopus:

1. Trust the process. The octopus's lack of proprioception means it must rely on the mini-brain to perform its specialized function. Therefore, it will experience most things before it sees it. In fact, the experience may shape the vision.

2. Trust your team. The octopus has only two eyes and eight arms. It cannot see what all eight arms are doing at the same time all of the time, so it must trust its team of specialized neurons that control each arm.

3. Remove then regenerate. Whether trying to escape a predator or in case of injury or disease, octopuses have been known to sever their own arms. This biological phenomenon is called autophagy. The octopus does not worry about losing a limb that could render it defenseless. After all, the octopus has the ability to close its own wound and regenerate a new arm. We must be

willing to recognize parts of our lives that hinder us from reaching our fullest potential.

4. Be nimble. *National Geographic* has a video that shows a 600-pound octopus squeezing through a tube the size of a quarter. Octopuses have no bones. The hardest part of their body is their beak. Therefore, if the beak fits, it fits. We should be as malleable and adaptable as the octopus. Whether the job market or stock market, entrepreneurial landscape or environmental landscape, change is certain. Flexibility and adaptability are skills to ensure survival of them all.

5. Be a self-starter and an independent learner. Shortly after the male octopus mates, he dies. Similarly, the female octopus dies after her eggs hatch. So, baby octopuses come into the world essentially without parents. Everything they learn is gained from their own experiences. However, we have learned that the octopus is highly intelligent with its nine "brains" that control movement, taste, and feel. It also learns from its environment via the 240-plus suckers on each arm, totaling over 2,000. These suckers assist with taste, smell, and grasping objects. There are reports of octopuses studying objects and quickly

learning to use them, from opening pill bottles to using coconut shells for shelter.

From its ability to move gracefully through the water, to its movement coordinated by the two-thirds of its nervous system located outside of its head, to regenerating a new appendage, fitting into the smallest of spaces, and learning to use tools in its environment, the octopus is a highly intelligent and remarkable creature. And to think, it does these things from day one of its life without wisdom passed down from dear old Mom or Dad.

Taking a note from this creature of wonder, we must trust our instincts, be adaptable, and embrace lifelong learning.

References

1. U.S. Bureau of Labor Statistics. "Employee Tenure Summary." Accessed March 28, 2020.

2. Massachusetts General Hospital. "Physicians less likely than other health professionals to be divorced, study finds." ScienceDaily. www.sciencedaily.com/releases/2015/02/150218141315.htm. Accessed April 11, 2021.

3. Quotes.net, STANDS4 LLC, 2021. *"Michael Jordan Quotes."* Accessed May 16, 2021. https://www.quotes.net/quote/61001.

About the Author

Terralon Cannon Knight, MD, is a board-certified family physician, speaker, author, and sought-after career transition coach. A native of Macon, Mississippi, she has a passion for the underserved, with much of her career spent aiding communities in the District of Columbia, Maryland, and Virginia.

Dr. Terralon is a graduate of Tougaloo College, where she was recognized in the Tougaloo College Inaugural Class of 40 under 40 and inducted into the Tougaloo College Alumni Hall of Fame. She obtained her medical degree from the Warren Alpert Medical School of Brown University and completed her family medicine residency at University of Texas at Houston. As the principal of Knight Coaching, LLC, Dr. Terralon helps physicians make pivotal career changes in order to create more freedom, flexibility, and financial independence.

Dr. Terralon resides in Upper Marlboro, Maryland, where she enjoys traveling, photography, and her favorite pastimes––serving as chauffeur, chef, and personal assistant to her three children.

Learn more at www.drterralon.com